From Zero to Hero:

The definitive manual for establishing
a prosperous online business.

Daniel L. Brent

Table of contents

Introduction

Starting an online company may be an enormously gratifying undertaking, but it can also be intimidating and hard. Without a solid basis, your firm may struggle to develop momentum, and you may find yourself spinning your wheels without seeing any progress.

In this chapter, we will cover the significance of creating a strong foundation for your online business and give ideas on setting goals and developing a business strategy.

The Importance of Setting Goals.

Before you begin establishing your online business, it is crucial to have clear goals for what you want to achieve.

These goals will act as a roadmap for your business, helping you stay focused and motivated.

Setting objectives can help you define your vision and determine what activities you need to take to accomplish your desired end.

When defining objectives, it's crucial to make them precise, measurable, attainable, relevant, and time-bound.

For example, instead of stating a generic aim like "make money online," you may create a precise objective like "earn $5,000 per month within six months by selling digital products."

Setting SMART objectives can help you stay focused and motivated. You will be able to track your progress and make modifications in future to guarantee you are on track to attaining your objectives.

Developing a Business Plan.
Once you have determined your goals, the following stage is to construct a business strategy.
A business plan is a written document that details your business goals, strategies, and techniques for accomplishing those goals. It acts as a roadmap for your firm, helping you stay focused and make smart decisions.

Your business strategy should include the following elements:

Executive Summary: A quick description of your firm, including your mission statement, product offers, target market, and goals.

Market examination: A complete examination of your target market, including demographics, buying patterns, and pain areas.

Products and Services: Description of your products and services, including price, features, and advantages.

Marketing Strategy: A thorough plan for reaching your target audience, including social media marketing, email marketing, content marketing, and other approaches.

Financial Projections: A prediction of your income, costs, and cash flow for the first three to five years of your organization. By drafting a business plan, you'll have a clear roadmap for your firm, making it simpler to make strategic decisions and stay focused on your goals. It will also help you identify possible barriers and plan how to overcome them.

Setting a firm foundation is vital for the success of any online business. By creating clear goals and constructing a business plan, you will have a roadmap for your firm, making it simpler to make smart decisions and stay focused on your goals. In the next chapters, we will discuss the numerous facets of starting an online business and present advice for success.

Whether you are just starting or trying to take your business to the next level, a strong foundation is the key to reaching your objectives and developing a thriving online business.

Identifying Your Niche

When launching an online business, identifying your specialty is one of the most critical steps toward building a successful and profitable operation.

A niche refers to a specialized area of interest or expertise that you choose to focus on within your sector.

By selecting a niche that matches your interests and abilities, you will be able to establish yourself as an authority in that field and offer products and services that meet the unique demands of that market.

Assess Your Interests and Expertise.

The first step in identifying your specialty is to assess your hobbies and expertise. Take time to reflect on your passions, hobbies, and abilities. Consider the subjects that you are informed about and have a natural tendency towards.

When establishing a specialty, it is vital to find an area that corresponds with your interests and expertise. If you're passionate about the issue, you'll be more motivated to develop high-quality content and products that resonate with your audience. Your expertise in the niche will also assist identify you as a reputable authority, which is vital for generating trust with your audience.

Research Your Market.
Once you have a few ideas for your niche, it's time to explore your market. Your goal is to assess whether there is sufficient demand

for the items or services that you propose to offer.

Start by using keyword research tools like Google Trends and Keyword Planner to evaluate the search volume and competitiveness for phrases related to your niche.
High search traffic and low competition suggest that there is demand for your products or services, but there is not much competition.
Learn from your competition to grasp their strategy, products, and services.
Analyze their social media profiles, websites, and blog posts to determine how they advertise themselves and communicate with their audience.

By studying what your competitors are doing, you may identify how you can differentiate yourself and build a value offer for your audience.

Narrow Down Your Niche.
Once you have done your first research, it's time to narrow down your niche. Look for places inside your expertise where you have a unique angle or perspective that sets you apart from the competitors.
For instance, if you are a fitness specialist, you could limit yourself to a field like yoga or high-intensity interval training.

By narrowing down your niche, you will establish yourself as an authority in that area and offer products and services that match the specific demands of your target market.

When you focus on a topic, you will be able to differentiate yourself from competitors who may have a broader concentration.

Test Your Niche.

Before committing to your niche, it is vital to test it out. You can achieve this by producing a minimum viable product (MVP) and launching it to a limited group of people to receive feedback.

An MVP is the most basic version of your product or service which you may deliver to your target customer.

For example, if you are establishing an online course, you could create a short teaser film and offer it to a select number of people to test interest.

This input can help you tweak your product and confirm the demand before spending too much time and money into it.

Identifying your specialization is a vital step in developing a successful online business. By examining your hobbies and experience, researching your market, narrowing down your niche, and testing it out, you'll be able to locate the perfect market for your business and produce products and services that match the specific demands of your target audience.

As you move forward with your specialization, continue to study and enhance your techniques.

Regularly assess your competitors and stay up-to-date on industry developments to stay ahead of the curve.

Creating a Memorable Online Presence

In today's congested online industry, having a strong brand is crucial to separate from the competition and establish credibility with your audience. Your brand is more than simply a logo or a name; it is the core of your business and the values that it symbolizes.

We will cover the steps to grow your brand and create a memorable online presence.

Define Your Brand Identity.

The first step in developing your brand is to define your brand identity.

Your brand identity is a visual and vocal representation of your firm, including your logo, color scheme, message, and tone of voice.

Start by establishing your brand's mission, beliefs, and personality.

What do you want to achieve with your business, and what ideals do you wish to embody? How do you want your audience to perceive you? These questions will help you build your brand identity and create a consistent and unified brand across all your online channels.

Create Your Visual Identity.

Once you have identified your brand identity, it is time to create your visual identity. It comprises your logo, color palette, typography, and other components that represent your business.

When designing your visual identity, examine your target demographic and what will resonate with them.

Choose colors and fonts that reflect your brand's personality and beliefs.

Your logo should be simple, distinctive, and easy to recognize. All visual aspects should be consistent throughout all your online channels, including your website, social media profiles, and marketing materials.

Craft Your Brand Message.

Your brand message is the language and tone of voice you employ to communicate with your audience.

It should reflect your brand's personality and beliefs and resonate with your target audience.

When designing your brand message, it is crucial to consider your target audience's pain points and desires.

What challenges are they trying to solve, and how can your firm help them?

Go straight to the point, and avoid jargon or technical phrases your readers may not comprehend.

Create a Content Strategy.

A good content strategy is vital to creating your brand and establishing credibility with your audience.

Your content strategy should align with your brand identity and message and deliver value to your target audience.

Start by outlining your content goals and the themes you wish to cover. Then, construct a content calendar and plan out your material in advance.

Use a mix of forms, including blog entries, videos, social media postings, and email newsletters, to engage with your audience and develop an online presence.

Engage with Your Audience.

Engaging with your audience is crucial in building a brand and generating trust with your audience.

Respond swiftly to comments and messages on your social media pages and website.

Use social media to create discussions with your audience and seek feedback on your products and services.

Developing your brand is a vital step towards achieving a successful online business.

By defining your brand identity, creating your visual identity, crafting your brand messaging, creating a content strategy, and engaging with your audience, you will be able to create a memorable online presence and establish credibility with your target audience.

Continue to monitor and refine your strategies.
Regularly assess your audience and change your message and content to match their growing needs.
In the next chapter, we will cover the importance of developing an email list and how to accomplish it efficiently.

Designing an Effective Online Storefront

In today's digital age, your website is your storefront. It is the first impression your audience will have of your business, and it is crucial that it represents your brand and provides a seamless user experience.

In this chapter, we will discuss the procedures to construct a website that represents your brand and effectively promotes your products or services.

Step 1: Define Your Website Goals
Before designing your website, it is crucial to outline your goals. What do you want your website to achieve? Do you want to sell

products, create leads, or provide information about your services?

Defining your website goals will help you identify the layout, content, and design aspects needed to fulfill those goals.

Step 2: Choose a Platform
There are various website platforms, including WordPress, Shopify, and Wix, each has features and perks, so choose one that suits your website goals and budget.

Consider considerations like the simplicity of use, customization choices, and security features when picking a platform.

Step 3: Plan Your Website Architecture
Your website architecture is the framework of your website and pages.

Prepare your website architecture in advance to guarantee that it is easy to navigate for your audience.

Start by generating a sitemap that outlines the pages and components of your website. Group relevant pages together and prioritize the most important pages, such as your homepage and product pages.

Step 4: Design Your Website
Your website design should coincide with your business identity and deliver a seamless user experience.
When building your website, consider things like font, color scheme, and layout.
Use high-quality photographs and graphics to display your products or services, and

ensure that your website is suited for mobile devices.

Step 5: Create Compelling Content
Compelling content is vital to attract and engage your audience. Your website content should be useful, entertaining, and relevant to your target audience.

Start by designing a homepage that introduces your brand and provides an outline of your products or services. Use product descriptions and reviews to promote your offers, and include a call-to-action on each page to boost conversions.

Step 6: Optimize Your Website for SEO
Search engine optimization (SEO) is vital to drive organic traffic to your website.

Optimizing your website for SEO incorporates aspects including keyword research, on-page optimization, and link building.

Research keywords relating to your products or services, then incorporate them into your website text and meta tags.
Ensure that your website is structured and labeled correctly, and establish backlinks to your website to increase your search engine rating.

Step 7: Launch and Maintain Your Website
Once your website is built, launch it and update it periodically.
Test your website extensively to be sure it is running accordingly, and monitor its performance often to spot any concerns.

Update your website material to keep it new and current, and guarantee it is secure by periodically updating your security features and backing up your website data.

Building a website is a vital step towards developing a successful online business. By defining your website goals, choosing the right platform, planning your website architecture, designing a visually appealing website, creating compelling content, optimizing your website for SEO, and launching and maintaining your website, you will be able to create a seamless user experience and effectively showcase your products or services.
As time goes, continue to analyze its performance and make improvements as necessary.

In the next chapter, we will cover the importance of social media marketing and how to use it successfully to promote your brand.

Creating Products That Sell

Developing things that sell is a critical component of building a successful online business.

In this chapter, we will discuss the processes to produce items that align with your brand and suit the demands of your target customer.

Step 1: Define Your Product Niche.

Before generating items, it is crucial to determine your product niche. What things will you sell? What problem do they solve? Who is your target audience?

Defining your product niche will help you design items targeted to your audience's demands and tastes.

Step 2: Conduct Market Research.

Market research is vital to identify your audience's demands and preferences.

It entails analyzing market trends, customer behavior, and competition products.

Start by identifying your top competitors and studying their items and price.

Use consumer surveys and feedback to get an insight into your audience's wants and preferences.

Step 3: Create a Product Plan.

Creating a product plan entails determining the product characteristics, pricing, and launch strategy.

Consider production costs, projected profit margins, and deadlines while establishing your product plan.

Create a timeline that describes the production and launch milestones, and develop a budget that accounts for manufacturing costs, marketing, and any other expenses involved with product development.

Step 4: Create Your Products.
Once your product plan is in place, it is time to create your products.
Consider variables like materials, design, and packaging while designing your products.

Ensure that your products are of good quality and correspond with your brand identity.
Use consumer feedback and market research to enhance your products and

guarantee that they fit the demands and preferences of your target audience.

Step 5: Test Your Products.
Testing your products is vital to guarantee that they fulfill your quality requirements and connect with your brand identity. Consider organizing focus groups or beta testing to obtain input and discover any faults with your products.
Use customer input to develop your items and make any necessary adjustments before launching them to the public.

Step 6: Launch Your Products.
Launching your products requires building a marketing strategy and pushing your products to your target audience.

Consider employing a variety of marketing platforms, including social media, email marketing, and influencer collaborations, to reach your target demographic.

Develop product descriptions that highlight the characteristics and benefits of your items, and utilize high-quality photographs and videos to promote your offerings.

Step 7: Monitor and Refine Your Products.
After launching your items, monitor their performance and make any necessary refinements.
Use client feedback to detect any flaws and make improvements as necessary.

Continuously refine your products to ensure that they fit the demands and tastes of your target audience, and produce new products to expand your offerings and attract new customers.

Developing things that sell is a critical component of building a successful online business.

By defining your product niche, conducting market research, creating a product plan, creating high-quality products, testing your products, launching your products, and monitoring and refining your products, you will be able to build products that align with your brand and meet the needs and preferences of your target audience.

As you continue to create your products, use client input and market research to refine your offerings and ensure they remain relevant and competitive.

In the next chapter, we will cover the importance of customer service and how to deliver outstanding service to your customers.

Promoting Your Products and Brand

Marketing your business is vital to acquire new customers and promote your products and brand.

In this chapter, we will discuss the many marketing tactics you may employ to promote your business and reach your target audience.

Step 1: Define Your Marketing Goals.
Before designing your marketing strategy, it is necessary to outline your marketing goals. What do you hope to achieve with your marketing efforts? Do you want to improve sales, build brand awareness, or promote new products?

Defining your marketing goals will help you design a targeted marketing plan that aligns with your business objectives.

Step 2: Identify Your Target Audience.
Identifying your target demographic is vital to design marketing efforts that resonate with your audience's requirements and preferences.
Use market research and consumer surveys to get your audience's demographics, interests, and behavior.
Develop buyer personas to represent your ideal customer, and use them to influence your marketing message and approach.

Step 3: Develop a Marketing Plan.
Creating a marketing plan requires establishing the marketing channels and

methods you will utilize to reach your target audience.

Consider your budget, target audience, and marketing goals while establishing your marketing plan.

Use marketing platforms, including social media, email marketing, content marketing, and advertising, to reach your target audience and promote your products and brand.

Step 4: Create Compelling Marketing Content.

Creating captivating marketing material is vital to attract and engage your target audience.

Develop high-quality content that shows your products and brand and connects with your marketing goals and target audience.

Use high-quality photographs and videos to promote your products and generate educational and entertaining content that resonates with your target audience's interests and preferences.

Step 5: Measure and Analyze Your Marketing Performance.

Measuring and analyzing your marketing success is vital to understand what is working and what is not and making modifications as necessary.

Use marketing analytics tools to track your website traffic, social media engagement, and email marketing performance.

Use this data to find areas for improvement, adjust your marketing strategy, and optimize your marketing efforts for success.

Step 6: Continuously Refine Your Marketing Strategy.

As you implement your marketing plan, consistently modify your approach to ensure it coincides with your marketing goals and resonates with your target audience.

Use client feedback and market research to discover what needs improvement and make adjustments as necessary.

Marketing your business is vital to acquire new customers and promote your products and brand. By defining your marketing goals, identifying your target audience, developing a marketing plan, creating compelling marketing content, measuring and analyzing your marketing performance, and continuously refining your marketing strategy, you will create effective marketing campaigns that resonate with your audience and drive business growth.

As you develop your marketing plan, experiment with different marketing channels and methods to determine what works best for your organization.
In the next chapter, we will cover the importance of customer service and how to deliver outstanding service to your clients.

Tracking Your Income and Expenses

Managing your finances is a vital component of establishing a successful online business.

By keeping track of your income and expenses, you should be able to make informed decisions regarding your business's financial health and prepare for long-term growth.

We will study how to manage your finances and track your income and expenses.

Step 1: Establish a Financial System.

The first step in managing your finances is to build a financial system.

This system should contain an accounting program or spreadsheet to track your income, expenses, and bank account. Getting a dedicated bank account and credit card for your business guarantees that your personal and business money remain separate, simplifying tax filing and offering a clear picture of your business's financial health.

Step 2: Track Your Income.
Tracking your money entails recording all sources of revenue, including sales, commissions, and advertising income. Use your bookkeeping software or spreadsheet to record each transaction, along with the date, amount, and source of revenue.
Be sure to categorize your income by product, service, or revenue stream to get a

clear sense of where your revenue is coming from.

Step 3: Record Your Expenses.
Recording your expenses requires documenting all costs for running your business, including supplies, equipment, advertising, and other expenses.
Use your bookkeeping software or spreadsheet to record each transaction with date, amount, and purpose.

Be sure to categorize your spending, such as advertising, supplies, or rent, to get a clear sense of where your money is going.

Step 4: Reconcile Your Accounts.
Reconciling your accounts requires comparing your bank and credit card statements to your bookkeeping software or

spreadsheet to ensure that all transactions are accounted for and accurate.

This method ensures that your financial records are up-to-date and accurate and helps uncover discrepancies or errors.

Step 5: Create Financial Reports.
Creating financial reports entails using your bookkeeping software or spreadsheet to generate reports that provide insight into your business's financial health.
Financial reports include income, balance sheets, and cash flow statements.

Use these reports to acquire a comprehensive knowledge of your business's revenue and expenses, find areas for improvement, and make informed decisions about your business's financial future.

Step 6: Plan for Taxes.
Planning for taxes entails assessing your tax due and setting aside funds to cover your tax responsibilities.
Consult with a tax specialist to determine the appropriate tax rate for your firm, and verify that you are setting away enough funds to satisfy your tax liability.

Managing your finances is a vital component of establishing a successful online business.
By building a financial system, documenting your income and expenses, balancing your accounts, preparing financial reports, and budgeting for taxes, you will make informed

decisions about your business's financial health and plan for long-term growth.

Be careful to periodically evaluate your financial records and reports, and change your financial strategy when necessary to ensure your firm remains profitable and financially healthy.

In the next chapter, we will study how to properly manage your inventory and guarantee that you have the right products to fulfill client demand.

Growing Your Business for Long-Term Success

Once you have created your online business and achieved initial success, it is time to start thinking about long-term growth and scalability.

In this chapter, we will discuss how to effectively scale your business and ensure it continues to expand and prosper over the long run.

Step 1: Assess Your Current Operations. The first step in scaling your firm is to review your present operations and find areas for improvement. Consider the following questions:

Are your present procedures and systems scalable, or will they need adjustments as your firm grows?

Is your present team equipped to meet growing demand, or will you need to acquire extra staff?

Are your present products and services in high demand, or do you need to increase your offerings to suit customer needs?

Do you have the financial resources to invest in expansion, such as marketing, new products, or equipment?

By answering these questions and finding areas for improvement, you should build a plan for scaling your firm effectively.

Step 2: Develop a Growth Strategy.

Once you have reviewed your current operations, it is necessary to establish a

growth strategy that will help you to fulfill your long-term business goals.
Consider the following strategies;

Expand your product or service offers; If your present offerings are in high demand, consider expanding your product or service line to reach new clients and markets.

Invest in marketing; Increase your marketing efforts to reach a wider audience and attract more visitors to your website.

Optimize your website; Improve your website's design, user experience, and functionality to increase conversions and generate revenue.

Hire additional staff; If your current workforce is stretched thin, consider recruiting more staff to accommodate rising demand and assist business growth.

Invest in new equipment or technology; Upgrade your equipment or technology to boost efficiency and increase capacity. By defining a growth strategy that corresponds with your long-term business goals, you should be able to make informed decisions about how to scale your organization effectively.

Step 3: Monitor Performance Metrics.
It is necessary to evaluate performance data consistently.
Consider the following metrics:

Revenue growth; Track your revenue growth over time to ensure your business is developing.

Conversion rate; Monitor your website's conversion rate to guarantee that your marketing and website optimization efforts are effective.

Customer acquisition cost; Calculate your customer acquisition cost to guarantee that your marketing efforts are cost-effective and sustainable.

Customer retention rate; Monitor your customer retention rate to verify that your firm is maintaining clients.

By analyzing these performance metrics periodically, you should be able to make wise decisions about how to alter your growth strategy and guarantee that your firm is developing sustainably and profitably.

Step 4: Continuously Improve Operations.

As your business continues to develop, it is crucial to consistently optimize your processes to guarantee that you are working at optimum efficiency.

Consider the following strategies: Streamline processes; Look for chances to streamline your operations and reduce inefficiencies slowing down your firm.

Implement new technology; Invest in new technology or software to enhance efficiency and automate monotonous operations.

Train staff; Provide regular training and support to your personnel to ensure they can handle rising demand and support business growth.

By consistently enhancing your processes, you will be able to ensure that your firm is working at optimum efficiency and prepared to meet growing demand as it continues to grow.

Scaling your firm is a vital component of achieving long-term success.

By reviewing your current operations, defining a growth strategy, monitoring performance metrics, and continuously improving your services, you will be able to scale your business successfully and ensure that it continues to expand and prosper over the long haul.

Taking Action and Building Your Dream Business

Congratulations! You have made it through the entire tutorial.

You now have the information and resources to start your dream online business.

While it may feel overwhelming, remember that many successful businesses have begun from the same spot as you and have gone on to achieve great things.

In this last chapter, we will highlight some of the insights from this course and provide some extra recommendations to help you get started on the path to success.

Take Action

The most important thing you can do now is to take action. All the knowledge and planning in the world won't matter if you don't put it into practice. The first step is always the hardest but also the most vital.

Start by defining goals for yourself and take steps to achieve them.
It could be registering your domain name or designing a logo for your brand.
Once you start making progress, it will become easier to stay going.

Keep Learning

The online business environment is continuously growing, so it's crucial to maintain learning and stay up-to-date with the latest trends and ideas.

Join online forums and groups, attend webinars and conferences, and study books and articles on topics relating to your field.

Network

Building ties with individuals in your sector is another crucial component of building your business.

Attend local events, join online groups, and interact with other entrepreneurs through social media.

You never know where your next cooperation or relationship could come from.

Evaluate and Adjust

As your firm expands, it is crucial to analyze your progress and adapt your plans accordingly.

Keep track of your money, examine your marketing activities, and monitor customer feedback to remain on target.

Believe in Yourself
Building a successful online business takes time, hard work, and devotion.
There may be hurdles and disappointments along the path, but the most important thing is to trust in yourself and your vision.
Surround yourself with positive influences and ask for help when necessary.

In conclusion, developing a successful online business takes time, work, and dedication.
But with the correct mindset, education, and resources, you can make your idea a reality.

Remember to take action, keep learning, network, assess and adjust, and most importantly, believe in yourself.
Good luck with your entrepreneurial adventure!